COUNTERPANE

POEMS AND DRAWINGS

For Pauline Shapiro

Catherine Bates

Nov 3 / 94

Counterpane

POEMS AND DRAWINGS

CATHERINE BATES

LANSDOWNE HOUSE

Lansdowne House   222 Melville, Suite 16,
                   Westmount, Québec.   H3Z 2J5

Cover painting: Red Quilt No. 1
               by Catherine Bates

Book Design: Glen Williams

The publisher wishes to acknowledge
the editorial assistance of Anne McLean.

Canadian Cataloguing in Publication Data

Bates, Catherine, 1934–
  Counterpane

ISBN 0-920549-00-4

I. Title.

PS8553.A826C69 1984   C811'.54   C84-090214-X
PR9199.3.B38C69 1984

For my parents and their families

Grieves
Snyder
Bowen
Young

CONTENTS

In watching Catherine Bates change and develop as an artist over the past dozen years I've been struck in particular by two qualities. The first is the increasing attention paid to the particular and the personal as opposed to the general—the realization that the universal is after all best sought in the particular.

The first works of hers that I saw were the stylized little aluminum people, her version I imagine of the faceless, alienated, industrialized modern man we heard so much about in those days, though actually the Bates' version had an appealing touch of toy-like humour. But in any case she apparently decided that non-depersonalized humanity was more interesting, for soon after she showed the impressive portraits of family members. I remember in particular the portraits of her mother and father and elderly aunts, works which were marked by a searching gaze into the subject's humanness. Interestingly, some of her most compelling paintings were those of older people, and the same is true of the poems.

This search for essences was accompanied by the second quality, a quest for an exactness of expression—not to be confused with a literalness of depiction. This habit of seeking precision was especially striking in the art criticism she wrote for the Montreal Star in the early seventies. One of the things that always impressed me was her unwillingness to use the convenient familiar phrases to sum up the effect an art work had on her. Instead she was more likely to let you follow the process of her response, pointing out her own biases where she was aware of them and examining her reactions.

I don't have the same familiarity with her poems as I do with her criticism and visual art work. However, on reading them I was again aware of the insistence on the personal and particular (and I think she's best when she's not generalizing) and in the search for precision of expression, the search for the point at which the image speaks for itself without need of further elaboration.

Virginia Nixon

THE POEM'S THERE, SOMEWHERE

The poem's there, somewhere, I said,
and picked away debris.
I carted loads of it,
dug down and down, and all along the way
ideas were freed which lay asleep,
protected from the light of day.
I damned the task occasionally,
and wondered how on earth such words,
such simple little words,
all short,
could get themselves,
all by themselves,
so hidden, buried, oh so deep,
in reinforced concrete.

At last came time for smaller tools
to brush the bits away,
revealing to my eyes the bones of something
searched for all my life.
Slowly now,
respecting fragile age,
the fragments were exposed,
were seen to lie strung out
in careful combinations, all arranged.
In the hardest land on earth
I'd dug my grave,
and as it opened up,
all shining white, I saw
some little lines of words.

September 1977

ON BOARD SHIP

Combined in long metal-lined
boxes around the floating
lounge and reading room
of the transatlantic liner,
a jumble of rubber plants, ferns,
spider plants, intertwined vines.

They're clearly out of place.
It's not just
nationalities unknown,
names irrelevant.
They're caged,
sail dumbly, port to port,
back and forth,
trapped atop an
alien slippery surface.
Spilling waves lash
sometimes, splash
windowed plants.

Inside the salty glass
they seem so sad to me,
bits of growing green
marooned on Noah's ark.
They'll never disembark.
They're stuck.
They'll decorate or die,
be ignored, thrown overboard—
victims of a transplantation
ridiculous, absurd.

We can have more choice,
grow that extra sense
of when a place is right,
choose options to resist.

For us it's possible
to drift for short times,
occasionally,
and root, somewhere,
long enough
to bloom.

Aboard 'Stefan Batory'
August 1980

GARDEN WELL: Oxford Allotments

They go back instead to the old well
with the rusted corrugated cover.
Deep into darkness they lower
the dented pail,
and snap the rope,
feel the filling.

The new arrangement of piped-in water
isn't working just quite right
it seems; they say the taps
aren't all connected,
the flow of water
a sickly trickle.

They want the new convenience of course,
formally voted the application,
sent complaints to city council
of painfully silly
slowness to grant
a reasoned request.

But plastic pipes looked alien, strange,
black on arrival for burial,
all sprawled limp, codes stamped
on dead snakes;
and the brass fixtures
were far too shiny.

Nature will season the newness in time;
deep-creased hands will soften
the gloss on taps, and the tubes
will settle in earth.
And in late summer
the well will run dry.

In the meantime, the weathered rope on the pail
feels good, the stone-lined blackness
echoes, and entering its depths
they sense the mystery
that beckons them back
to the gardens in spring.

January 1981

THE HILLS

The tops of Dorset hills seem flat
for hills, and long, blending ends
with neighbours on each side to cup
the gentle valleys. Windows look up
from human flint-built nests to see
the cattle, black and white on green,
distance-calm in verdant pastures
between the farms. In nearby fields
the new-clipped sheep seem bright, big-eared,
white oval clumps with toothpick legs
threading their way across the patterned
prehistoric barrowed ridges.
Far trees break into sky,
birds cluster in protecting bunches,
hedgerows angle sloping land.
It's now the time of elder-blooms, wild roses,
foxglove. And haying, when, rolling over
the lines of hills and into the valleys,
low clouds give way to blue and sun,
greens and rusts and snapping dry grass.

Dorset, 1980

DRAWING, TOUCHED BY HAND

Drawing, touched by hand, is what
I live with, how I feel about
a tree, a flower, youth and age,
the sun, the guns and ammunition.

Drawing is this driving need to take
constructions of the world apart,
to make by hand some other different
combinations of reality. Difficult.

To begin, a sorting of ideas,
feelings, so closely knit they form
a wall of wanting, unfinished between
the head and heart, waiting for a hand.

It's risk, destroys accustomed comforts,
for nothing more than unstrung strands
and bumpy lines, the crude attempts
that jerk across the chasm to creation.

But drawing shows me how things work,
the hands that felt the making of the world,
the thrusting miracles of pleasure that happen
when head and heart are touched by hand.

Oxford
June–July 1980

ROSE AT BROADWATER COTTAGE

An opened rose is swelling
sweetness in a windowed glass
of water, soft against
the peeling sash and silent
waving grass behind.

No jostling for attention,
no clamouring of colour;
just pastel pinks, grey paint,
and sandy-coloured seeds;
and something almost secret.

In the spaces we look through
to see the solid things,
a fragile fragrance floats,
and fills transparent air,
and conquers us completely.

Dorset
July–August 1980

DRAWING NEAR WOODEATON

In February the sun shone in a warm spell
and I found my tree at a turning
towards Woodeaton.
Pollarded,
it scrambled for a sense of fullness;
bare-leaved,
it stored survival sap.
What was it made me stop?

Impatient lines on pages tumbled into rhythms.
Love let go enough, and we had fun, conspired
to nurture something new.
It took us days and days,
nine drawings, two paintings.
And then we stopped.

I don't know what kind of tree it is.
I keep meaning to go back and see a new spring leaf
and find it in a book. I never have.
The magic now is searching somewhere else.
But the drawings, paintings, still surprise me,
to think I held the pencil and the brush.

Oxford, 1980

CABBAGE

Today's plump cabbage was ready,
its outside slightly blighted, and bitten
by cabbage caterpillars now
nowhere in sight. The knife cut
across the stem, deciding quickly
that others would be left for seed.

Inside, I washed it, and sharpened yet another
knife to shred it into bits
that looked like food. Through the window
the bullocks played at goring, innocent,
their seeding rights decided long ago.
In man's nature, knives are necessary tools.

Devon, July 1980

BROADWATER COTTAGE

While I decide to rest, and float
away inside my sleepy head, I hear
a buzzing blue-backed fly inside
my quiet summer room. Trapped,
it frantically explores the limits
of its papered cage in space.

Memory stirs another fly
that searched in vain for a safe exit
over perfumed heads of flowers, people,
while yellowed heat through summer blinds
stilled the heavy air in a farm parlour
reserved for friends, and funerals.

Yes, it could be the same fly,
the same room buzzing in the heat,
the same buzzing in the same ears.
These sounds I hear in later life
fly inside a larger adult head,
ricochet, bounce off boney walls,
but all directions are the same.

I don't want to lie down any more.
My longest rest has not yet come.

Dorset, July 1980

THE ROSE

Age had paled the pink of the rose.
It was just picked yesterday,
and put in a glass jam jar
to grace the long-polished planks of table
where we ate. But pubescent
pinkish petals just curled tight
are now full open, a painter's 'contre
jour' delight, the edge lines white
to frame the inner clusters of wrinkles.
Visions vibrate. And suddenly I saw
it clearly, between my quiet early
morning entrance and the slowly growing
background hum of stirring bodies,
that age had paled the pink of my rose.

July 1980

MY AGED MOTHER GIVES ME A GIFT

My aged mother,
in an instant of touching,
gives me her gift.

I hold the book,
brown with colour and age,
and consider its inscription:

> James Jeffrey Stokes
> with kindest wishes on the oc-
> casion of his confirmation in Granthan,
> Parish Church, 19 Nov 1885 from
> Clement Elsmere
> Vicar of Spittlegate

Not even my family.

The Stokes lived down the road,
settlers come later with larger trunks
and room enough for books.
Milton's name I know
(probably son of James Jeffrey),
boyhood friend of my father, and link through whom
this book came to the Bowen family farm
on the St. Clair River
in Moore Township
early,
long before the shiny, reeking stacks of oil refineries,
and the yellow, choking haze of hydro plants,
before mercury-filled fish tainted the shore,
and before yellow-warm lights of long lake freighters
proved feeble competition
for those steady, white, unbudging fluorescents
of intruder factories, locking eyes landwards,
when once they had dreamed
to the headwaters.

I hold the book,
brown with colour and age,
and consider its cover.
Holy Communion it says, a whole book
that prepared them for saints and forgiveness of sins,
and filled them with all those other rolling rivers of phrases,
sheltering and strengthening and straightening them
in the hard ages, and legitimizing the work,
and the meanness
of the isolation.

The words echo now, for
James Jeffrey long gone, Milton too,
and Reginald Sebastian,
my father,
all of them gone and their time gone too,
the time when they treasured a
Preparation and Companion for Holy Communion,
a concept past meaning,
or maybe fulfilling—
for them.

I do not presume now
to come to this thy book
remembering words or cries and shouts
of joy and sorrow and sharing;
instead to spend my rituals
writing memoirs,
unspoken,
while the silent mouthing of my words
strains muscles of lips stretching
with increasingly frantic effort,
unprepared
for silence.

I hold the book,
brown with colour and age.
Ears are deaf, eyes are
blind, lips are stilled,

but through my hands I feel,
and strongly too,
the silent laying on of generations
of my people,
their holding of this book before me,
their communion.

Not just my family.

I am of them all,
whatever else.

I thank my mother.

May–October 1977

FOR MY MOTHER

I was eleven
pig-tailed and thin and blond-eyed
when my mother cut the bouquet
of white peonies, with a few red,
large, and wrapped
a wet napkin at the sliced stems, then all with
yesterday's newspaper, to make a cone-shaped
bundle of heavy perfume.

I was to hold it at the bottom and rest the top part
on my arm and take it two blocks down
the street to an old lady at number ten twelve
who sat in front of us at church with her mother,
both so old they looked like sisters,
the mother heavy with huffs and puffs and rouge,
the daughter always thinner and colourless,
daughter dying first in a mixed-up world.

Death made me hesitate
but she looks all right my mother said
and old people love children.
And so I went enjoying the going,
turning the flowers to smell the tops,
the sogging bottom diaper-wrapped,
then lifting the whole above my head like a
special something from God, the way
it was done in the church.
And I turned and watched someone strange walk
through the park, and danced over the lines
in the sidewalk, and arrived happy.

Peonies held by old hands have a special meaning now.
It has to do with smells of death fading away
from the flowers' fragrances, and the vision of
gnarled hands matching wrinkled lines of leaves
and petals of peonies, all complicated
and intricate in their larger boundaries.

I walked home quietly
and today, so long later,
I take my mother
a bouquet of peonies.

May 30–June 4, 1977

IN HER EIGHTY-SEVENTH YEAR

My mother was a most wise woman,
could tell the future from the past,
read tea-cups when it was the fashion,
chastised me for sharp edges that would hurt,
and said one day, 'No one in my family
knows when time has come to die.'

Now turned in bed according to the clock,
recumbent bowl tipped empty of great love,
filling fast with fluid and clear pity,
hating the white waiting, growing fast fears
falling deaf before Death's thick door,
piling up against the closing of long life.

We all feel terrible, visit sometimes,
but living afar, more often write notes
hoping nurses will read them as so much more
than just routine between pills, the changing
of beds, the turnings, and emptying of pans.
What can one do but wait for the final
heart-wrenching, blood-gurgling end.

Oxford
March–July 1980

THE HOSPITAL ROOM

Little books, sweet thoughts to tell,
  And cards, arranged with care,
From friends who always wished her well,
  And came sometimes to stare.

She valued the things in life she sensed
to be right, and it doesn't seem right that Death,
at the end, dallied and played long games.
But it's over. Take the things back, and cry.

There weren't many things left to take back,
at the end. She'd made sure of that,
not caring much for the clutter of life.
The body rolled out with only a tag;
she'd dispersed the other treasures she'd had.
Just books, cards, some photos, a comb.
She'd tried to explain it to us before,
'The first half of life's for gathering things;
the second's more fun, when you give them away.'

Her intuitions saw us far in life,
and later on she took the time
to write, when we'd all grown and gone
away. She always found a way
to say important things, without
a lot of words. She thought it was
profound to live each day. It now
would be appropriate if I
could mark the end with simple verse
and rhyme, an easy gait, and not
too hard to feel. But I'm a different
age; it doesn't come out that way.
She'll understand. She always did.

Oxford & Dorset
March–July 1980

A LETTER FROM OXFORD

I hear my rhythm fight against
the hum of tumbling drums of drying
clothes in the local launderama.
Dropped detergent speckles lint-
cocooned collections of candy wrappers,
kleenex bits, ends of cigarettes.

Clothes jounce, slip against glass;
regulars stare, judging suds; someone
folds hot underwear, his on top;
a couple necks; 'For Sale's outnumber
'Wanted's; the telephone's out-of-order.
It's all the same. Now where's my pen?

I slot the time between the drops
of silver coin to write home lines
I'd like to hear. Nothing about steady
rain, or the months of brussel sprouts.
No launderamas either. 'Dear Friend,
It's May. A sun-filled Saturday.'

Oxford
May–July 1980

WINDOW AT WYNFORD EAGLE

Grasstops fill with ripening seed,
budding thistle stems bend stiffly,
bushes, branches group with gusts,
just outside my window.

A fierce fighter on fast manoeuvers
dives the sunny hills to practise
corkscrew turns and keeps slick fit
in case it needs to kill.

The panes of glass around my mind
block the speeding scream; it fades
away, until mind's ear can hear
the sounds of grass again.

July 1980

AN ENDING HOME

Couched,
crouched almost,
shrinking daily
smaller
in the greyness
of the matching
moveable chair,
she sits and waits
for partner death
and cares
a little less
each shadowed day
for frills of life
and looks.

Her home of daily regimen
is planned for taking care
and quickly moving blurs of white
all speak as if to children, smiling,
and even try sometimes
to understand that ends
of life are naturally
quite ragged and unkempt.

September 9, 1977

KINDNESS HAS TWO EDGES

Poets praise flowers,
and everyone assumes
they should be loved.
But at the nursing home,
deposited on a summer porch,
they sit neglected and alone,
and inmates shun the heavy air
filled up with sweet perfumes.
Thoughtful nurses wait a while
to bring the baskets in, until
the stiffness of the stems subsides,
and they can rearrange, redress
and camouflage mementos from
a recent funeral rite.

What else to do? Leave
on the mound so many blooms
that waste is the memorial?
Recycle, don't discard!

But as we slice the stems
and cut the plots of earth
we hurt as well the human
remnants of our tidy lives,
and to those living, waiting,
bring flowering instructions
that remind them all again
their turn is next.

September 1977

WISHBONES

Soon afterwards,
we cleared the house
and came across
a cache of wishbones
in a bottom drawer
under patches of quilt
and stopped,
until one of us
laughed to cover
the question why.

Supposing she'd been
twenty-three, not ninety-three.
We'd have judged her
clever if she'd strung
some wishbone necklaces
on strong umbilical cords
for the new generation.
She'd have put in feathers,
the bones, blue beads and brass,
and let some leather of the thong
show knotted not too frequently,
finishing birthing of bones
with pride, seeing similarities
to those on brown bare breasts
in big anthropology books.

But she was ninety-three,
kept them all whispering
in the bottom drawer
underneath the quilt
where they didn't feel fears
that at an uncertain age,
embarrassed by exposure,
they'd be thrown into boxes
for dumping, and fly-away wishes
would helter-skelter scatter

to dark nooks and crannies
so they could stay safely
in the emptying house.

Long afterwards,
we felt her depths
of quirky talent
grafted on our bones,
alive in the heart
of the marrow's
imagination.

Rutherford, Ontario
1984

THE UNINVITED GUEST

Last night he dreamt they had a gala party,
But christened an unheralded event,
For in his dream he woke to see his love
Completely blinded in another love.
It seems they couldn't help themselves at all,
And touched and kissed their lips and hands so gently
That his heart was torn to memory's parts, in shreds,
And shrieks all silent lay all dead, stillborn.
Past their bodies sparkling with fresh love
He saw a window and old friends across the street
Who danced in honour of the Season's Child,
And busy, served their own invited guests.
He didn't ask for help, it was too late;
When love is born we only like to celebrate.

September 1977

AGAIN

Toenail clippings on bathroom broadloom
again.
You'd think he could pick them up.
Did he think to leave them there
to state his own priorities?
Or did he just not think at all
that someone, someone
has to bend their butt
to pick them up
again.

Dirty dishes in the cluttered kitchen
again.
You'd think she'd clean the house
and take some pride in her work.
Or does she just not think at all
that caring, caring
is what it's all about?
Like doing the dishes
again.

It's time they took a long vacation
again.
Not together, away from each other.
Do they think they can last for years
on a few old hackneyed dreams?
Or did they just not think at all
that sometimes, sometimes,
marriages get tired
and need a rest
again.

Oxford
February–July 1980

THE BEST LOVE

The best love lives a life that touches earth
without the knowing it is there, and real.
It grows a keenness, a wonder all its own.

Love is beauty in the sweetness of hay
that does not hear the coughing of cows
or smell the sharp ammoniac air.

Montreal
September 13, 1980

TWO THISTLEDOWNS

Two thistledowns take quiet flight
To catch each other's filaments
And softly whirl a silent round.

They dance and drift and touch again
To tangle silky whitened strands
And feel their newborn gentleness.

These thistledowns caress the breeze,
Then fast in love with all the world,
Float down to earth and quiet sleep.

September–October 1978

ON THE LAKE

I look down to the waters of this ancient lake,
And see reflections of myself distorted,
Tattered slipping pieces mirrored across
The endless waves of Narcissistic search,
Bouncing back broken, incomplete.
My look slips past this twisting glittering surface
To the clearness below the boat; it goes as far
As eye can see, that deepening fluid supporter
Of my boat and me; its dappled calm caresses,
gently fills my crevasses of care.
Then, when sense of goal comes back to me,
I straighten and look up, set myself on course,
Move ahead with measured speed and thrust,
And leave completed images of self to trust.

Oxford, August 1980

THIS APPLE TREE

This apple tree, half dead, alone,
saw my great grandmother, alive—
she did her washing by its side,
according to my father's memory.
(Her house that lived in front of it
now sits behind; wide roads of progress
pushed it back some twenty years ago.)
This tree's been pruned and cared for, but mostly
left alone to bear each year its fruit,
come heavy even now, with season's regularity.
This tree has seen more life than I shall see,
it knows more secrets, is more wise,
and I regard it with the love of many lives,
and it displays for me, each year, my heritage.

When levellers come to tear the house
up from its roots, and move away
the bones of what we called a home,
when holes that held picked apples and preserves
are all filled in and covered and smoothed,
and no one seems to know the difference
any more, I hope this tree still stands
for me to see as I pass by.
There must be something left
that dies a natural death, that lives out time
in rhythms and cycles, large approximates,
with countdowns imprecise, unmonitored.
I fear the powers of life's cruel enemies,
to see them cut this tree, and kill my memories.

September–October 1977

NOW

His mother's orders were final.
Drown the kittens before
they open their eyes.
Don't put it off.
Do it today.
Do it.

Now.

The grave came first, under barbed
wire beside the first field,
small and shallow and round,
not dead-drop cliffs at funerals
where right-angles cleared clay
straight down.

Strong brown burlap bag soft
with dust would do, and a string,
to be tied temporarily.
High-pitched never-ending mews
kept pace from barn to trough,
troubling talk.

Silence.

That thin-walled ragged metal trough
had ugly corrugated Death's ribs,
was rusty already;
a brute pipe without spigot
spurted water unevenly;
the bag gained soaking weight.

Sun splashed white
reflecting blue;
red-winged blackbirds chattered
extraordinarily loudly;

muted voices of imagination
discussed the test of time.

Too soon.

He had me hold them now. Now,
he could call me accomplice,
the price one pays to learn
about life. You have to satisfy
a how-is-it-done curiosity
about massacres of innocents.

We put earth on top of wet furs,
didn't mark the place,
walked away without words,
hung the bag upside down to dry,
leaned the shovel in a dark corner,
lunched with conflicted appetites.

Comes the end.

Unexpected exhumed memories
of age and contemplation
surprise me when
they put events together.
He drowned later in warm waters
off Bermuda, swimming.

1984

OBITUARIES

Each piece was neatly cut, a collection
put in a pile beside tools on a shelf
in the cold, private place where he puttered
and thought about life and stealthy death.

Many were old, yellowed and brittle,
two inches each of formula listings
with name, the date and place of death,
next of kin, where services would be held.

His I placed on top; then took
them all in my fist and threw them out.
Obituaries are dismal portraits, wordy,
and it's not yet time to count my friends.

October 1980

TRUMPETS CALLED ALL SILENT

Trumpets called, with multi-coloured visions
in wondrous royal array, and made the lengths
of dull school hours fade away in grey.
Those special trumpets, of a silent voice,
all grew on vines across one end of porch.
Each day in spring when end of classes came,
I hurried to my rendezvous to count the blooms
that fell to hard cement along the lane
beside the house. I found the freshest ones,
new-fallen, full of colour yet, sweet orange,
and slipped them on my fingers, small end out,
and let my mind run free to see this time
what I would be—magician, wicked witch,
a fighting Devil, or God's converted angel.

I'd flex those fingers to twice their normal length,
or point just one to beckon a wandering cloud,
slowly motioning to all my wishes and wants,
without a single sound to break the silence.
Powerful strengths came through those fragile tips,
and told me to take charge of destinies,
my own and others, then to bask in glory
as tapered hands acknowledged cheering crowds.
Such seasons are not long in childrens' lives.
Pollen-dusted petals wear out quickly when in use,
and some days it was difficult to find enough
to fit ten fingers grown accustomed to the best.
But worst of all were days of disappointment
when I came and saw them gone, all swept away.

September–October 1977

DAWN MILLS' CEMETERY

They've lined the stones up side by side,
Around their bases poured cement,
So we can see all standing straight,
Mementos long inscribed with names,
And dates.

The graves they headed sink behind,
And no one hears complaints, regrets
That old Aunt Rill or Uncle Will
Have unmarked plots to moulder in,
Alone.

Two pine trees guard the cross-road scene
Where horse-drawn hearses used to pass,
Their thin and ragged branches bent
To fit the winds, their trunks still straight,
Awhile.

When spaces one by one get filled,
Old stones show cracks, are tipped askew,
And graveyards die, and trees grow old,
And younger souls regroup the past,
Again.

Dawn Mills, Ontario
December 1977

BICKFORD, ONTARIO

Sometimes a place can change its chosen name,
And underneath the title stay the same.
But some names don't just change, they up and die,
And places disappear completely from the eye.
I know, quite well, a little village of this kind,
That settlers always dreamed and hoped they'd find;
Built near road and rail and river, it impressed
The careful builders with a future seeming blessed.
But though it had a birth to celebrate,
Its meagre growth remained in such a state,
Rejoicings were short-lived, and all too soon
It sickened, and the talk was full of doom.
As rich, good soil determines growth of plants,
Towns for people grow on more than chance.

I wonder, it might have done better with an odd bit of luck,
Or a crazy break in the game. But death's progress was struck;
It got ripped up, torn down, trucked out, levelled and covered,
And now on the land squats there for you to discover,
A fume-belching, foul-smelling fertilizer factory-whore,
That bags its excretions on the grave of the general store.

September–October 1977

I HAD A DREAM BEFORE WE SOLD THE FARM

I dreamt last night there was a gala party
at our Bowen family farm, with house and barn
outlined in neon lights, a tawdry dress,
to match the nearby river's sullied bib.
And at the barn's far end swayed back and forth
two hydro towers, wired to blast out beats
of crashing music pounding down the land.
While rhythms packed foul air inside, and stars
were pushed away to hide, the nearby whites
of factory lights, in crazy dance, all tried
to mate with yellow glows of river boats,
but sterile hopes knew well they had no chance.
    The once-clear waters, clogged with scummy waste,
    lapped the border farm, now all debased.

They came, long lines of cars, to celebrate,
but slowed to snaily pace, with headlights lit,
as to a funeral rite, except they honked
their brassy horns in pasture parking lots,
and spewed blue fumes, and didn't pay respects.
I feared to see these steady rolling streams
of shining limousines move in and down
the rutted lane, and tried to tell them all
they'd made a big mistake; the party must
be somewhere else along the river road.
A frantic brother blocked the entrance way,
but pushed aside, saw vulgar hordes crush by.
    The changes tolled a strange and raucous knell,
    And we all knew the baggage came from hell.

We listened, looked, and made one more attempt,
this time to rid the house too overflowed
and gauche, but spread about the gaudy rooms
were soft and puffy people, eyes glass-patched,
who rotted in upholstered chairs, and reeked
of progress. Hands shook hands and glasses clinked;
in fetid air shrill laughter cleared its throat;

but eyes were blind to wildly flailing arms,
and ears were deaf to pleading, anxious cries.
All torn from souls to save our century farm,
emotions gathered sadly in defeat,
to enter graves now open at their feet.
> The family said good-bye to treasured dreams,
> and buried them, well-wrapped in muffled screams.

September 11–November 14, December 31 1977

ON MY VISITS TO THE RIVER

At home, for visits on the St. Clair River's shore,
Reflecting water sparkled there, hour by hour,
Revealing wisdom's views and nature's vistas,
Inviting longer stays and days of love.

I planned the happy sojourns to fit the seasons,
To see the river change before my eyes,
And glisten white with ice or blue with waves,
To feel it lap my soul in harmony with times.

But times changed too. Slowly the river gave up
Its blue, and fields and skies were victimized
As factories sprawled across whichever way,
Discharging to the river all their sewer wastes.

> The family book said a hundred years and more
> Were vested in the land beside this shore.

Neighbours sold their farms and moved away,
And busy drones at factories turned their backs
On cutters keeping channels free from winter ice,
On poisoned waters too hot for cold-blood fish.

The river widened as waves rolled in and in,
And in again as ships increased their size;
When roots washed bare and no one seemed to care,
Green willows dipped their branches into death.

There's no one there to visit now, and sad
Laments are sung sometimes across the miles;
But shrieks are born and torn apart for rivers
Raped at will, and rendered impotent, and killed.

> Lift your eyes and see this sordid shore;
> Each day your once-proud river's soul dies more.

September 1977

ON PLANTS, IN CANS

She grows her plants in tomato cans
    Whose bottoms, punched with holes,
Sit side by side on assorted pans
    And saucers and small chipped bowls.

Fall window sills are crowded each year
    With haphazard homes of tin,
Each label left on as a souvenir,
    To yellow, like aging skin.

Winter wages long campaigns,
    And day retreats from night,
Transient snows battle transparent panes,
    And plants flaunt green at white.

People pass, full of plans,
    Then slow a bit to see,
Point to rusty tomato cans,
    As products of penury.

Our lady grows plants in tomato cans,
    Sets them out in spring,
Hears her wards give thanks to cans,
    And start their blossoming.

February 1978

MY VIEW

My house lies filed and numbered on a little hill,
a cube buried deep in sprawling city noise,
and yet a good choice in a world they say is bad.
Seen over a neighbour's garage, flat-roofed with tar,
between his aging peeling second floor
and the newest box of homely porched apartments,
I have my precious piece of distant view,
just inches (centimetres now) of leafy hills.
I look and dream and do my meditations there,
and know it is this window past the window of
my house that makes my daily rituals worth living.
But how I marvel from inside my city prison
that a little tiny cut-out section of horizon
is my greatest nourishment and treasured love.

September 1977

OZYMANDIAS REVISITED

The young Westmount lady
sat proper in the window
of the local junk store,
calmly embalmed in an old photo
selling for the price of the frame,
antique, gilt-edged.

Who would have thought
to see her here,
hands gently clasped,
pearls in place,
gazing with soulful eyes
past the tatters of neighbours.

The junk man took her out
and sold the frame.

Montreal
September 1977, 1984

RAMPANT POLLEN

When the rampant pollen of wild flowers
    floats to burnish my hair,
And sun-bright sky-filled warmth
    caresses the cares from my face,
I reach to touch the colours,
    and fall into the arms of the world.

New sounds arc the air,
invisible darts and dives,
a lilt, a swoop, a glide,
and all the sad laments subside.

Port au Persil, Quebec
July 18, 1981

COLOUR-THOUGHTS

Whether it's marigolds for funeral garlands,
origami phoenixes on black ash memories,
sparkling red wine, blood sun, blue sky,
tender greens or ripened russets,
we conspire with colours.

They cover darknesses
we might trip into, will someday,
when depths we try to avoid
will be natural to fall into,
holes in a pozos-spotted Mexican hill
overgrown with cacti and brown weeds
where we count the seconds till the stone
strikes the bottom—
and look at each other,
knowing the time will come.

Walking back, the sky is bluer, flowers larger,
stamens brighter, pistils strong, leaves so lush,
and now we see whole multicoloured rainbows
flick across the drops on the petals
in the watered garden.

January 1983

HOW CAN I PAINT WITH LOVE?

They shot Bernadette Devlin last night;
Le Devoir says so, front page news.
I can't resist the reading on
to find her "gravement blessée"
in body, arms and legs. I see
spilled red spreading in my mind.

I'm angry, deep and deeper down;
it's wrong to shoot, to maim,
no matter how hate happens.
And I resent the bald reports of acts
like this, the media's bland assumption
that facts are facts without effects.

For in my present anger how can I paint
with love that amaryllis brought last night,
full in bloom and regal on its stalk,
filling radiantly with unseen ripples
a space so many times its size.
How can I do it? How can I do it?

January 1981

70

THAT CAT IN THE PARK

Today I saw that cat again
in the park, in a patch
of grass between the tallness
of some trees and a trapped squirrel.
Dashings back and forth;
the cat pounced for the squirrel,
stole a look over its shoulder,
saw my dog and me, showed fear,
and I unleashed my dog.
Mad race to the wire fence;
the squirrel went through,
the cat climbed to the top,
the dog sniffed and lifted his leg.
I watched and wondered
if that was how great wars began,
wished that was how they ended.

September 1980

THE PARK MAN

The walk-to-work crowds
exercise in straight lines
on hard grey lengths of cement
and go past, heads down, not seeing
him jab at the crumpled bits,
keeping his Eden clean.

But we, we know each other,
for we have seen each other
turn away slowly
after stoppng to hear leaves grow,
after sending a smile to the flowers,
feet wet in the dew of the green green grass.

September 1980

REQUIEM FOR THE BIG-CAR MAN

In the first half of the twentieth century
big cars commanded respect, and got it.
People continued to love each other,
to wipe away tears and cheer success,
to work on their lives' assembly lines.
But respect was reserved for The Big-Car Man,
and we saw how often that car got washed,
and each night if he put it in his garage.
The colours varied—black, dark blue,
softening later to gun-metal grey—
all of them sombre, subdued it's true,
but our Big-Car Man had his point of view.
So when he died we came from afar,
to mourn the day they sold the car.

September 1977

RHYMES ROB SOMETIMES

Rhymes rob sometimes,
make whispers in ears
of words which should ring loud
and clear, gaily tossing
and dancing in the air,
fine-tuned to feelings
felt before chains locked.

Unrhymed, worn words relearn,
display primeval talent
and sound their trumpets once again
to waken ears
so lulled to sleep
by rhymes
which rob, sometimes.

September 1977

HOUSTON

Silkscreened autumn bush
deep in red
to match striped spreads
on beds, twin, lying
at attention, smoothed
and straight against
the coloured walls
in all three hundred rooms.

Pink sky behind this bush
and yellow ground, and orange,
the multi-coloured thirty-second
time that print was calculated,
registered exact,
co-ordinating to a room
designed to bleed us dry.

Houston
March 17 1978

PARTING

On the paths everyone walks,
twisted, paper-thin, transparent,
old crinkled bits of life
are shed, snake skins after struggle,
or blow away, autumn
leaves retreating before
the same wind that scattered
seeds.

They kissed an overdue goodbye,
the tenderest thing for years.
It's like that when you know it's over,
and the soft newness feels fresh,
fragile.

Oxford
June–July 1980

REMEMBERING

I long ago looked up and waved
from a quiet tree-lined hospital street,
past summer leaves in heat-bee dance
to a windowed white-gowned figure, thin.

To-day we stand on green green grass;
I tell young eyes that look like mine
of a touching ghost-like glimpse of love,
and feel her see me gowned in white.

August 1980

AMARYLLIS

Where are you going to go,
Scarlet Ludwig Amaryllis?

Flaming flower
four-winged
long-stalked
proud and
pushing hard
from bulbous
hairy roots.

You're bursting your blooms
and here are windows of all
main rooms cleared completely
so painters with smelly cans
and coveralls, brushes, tapes,
can drape huddles of furniture,
attack walls and window-sills,
repair nail holes and cracks,
brush on new colours, fresh,
above all clean and bright.

For you, another room—
spill your beauty there,
while we watch artificial
colours bleed on walls,
and wonder about choices.

1984

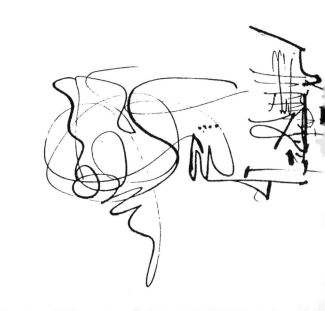